CATHY WILKES

Dear Viewer / Daor Breathnóir

My creations will occupy six rooms.

The smallest particle of suffering is the object, and I, the subject who acts upon the object,
am every atom unfolding from the womb. An atom here among us and another atom
in a faraway galaxy are inseparable epitomes of the same.

I solemnise and dignify the ghosts of interference which proceed from their origin and
whip themselves up before me. I observe, they nucleate and propagate. If I could disappear,
how fluid, how graceful and unending, how undisturbed and unpredictable would be the
changing patterns thereabout.

On both the left and on the right, there is nothing worth seeing and nothing worth hearing.
I return home to wait in place and draw forth what is yet to come.

CW

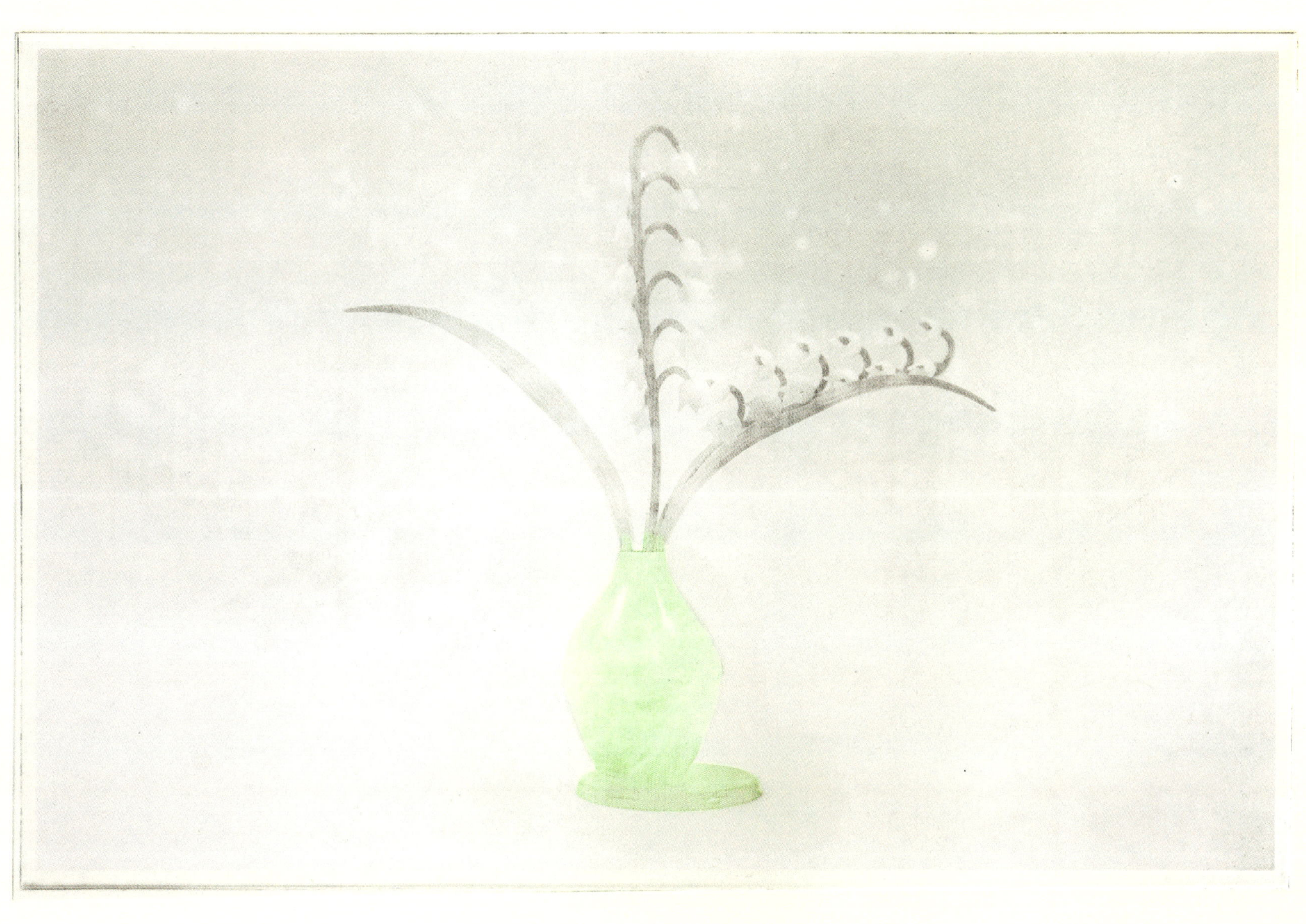

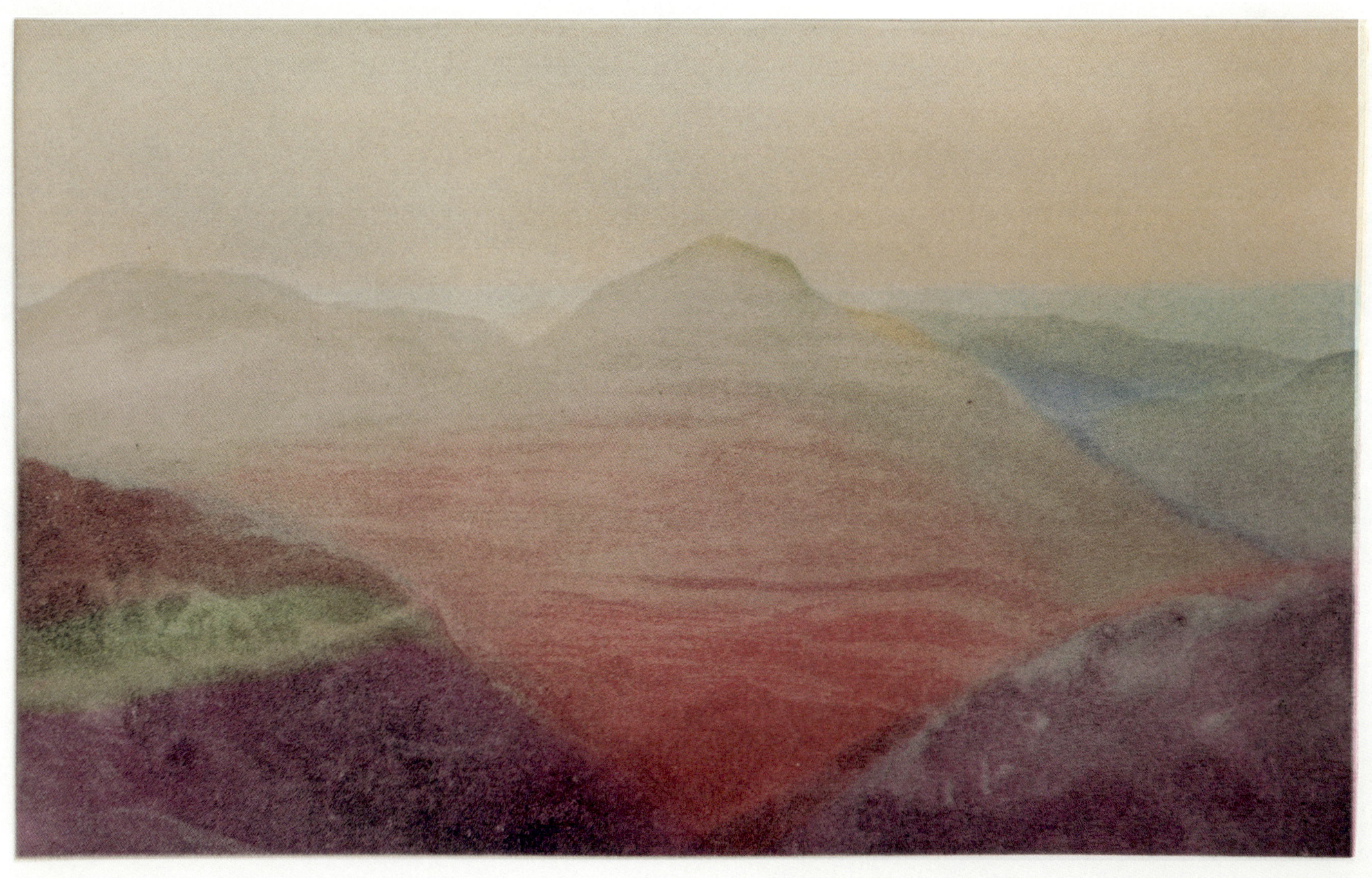

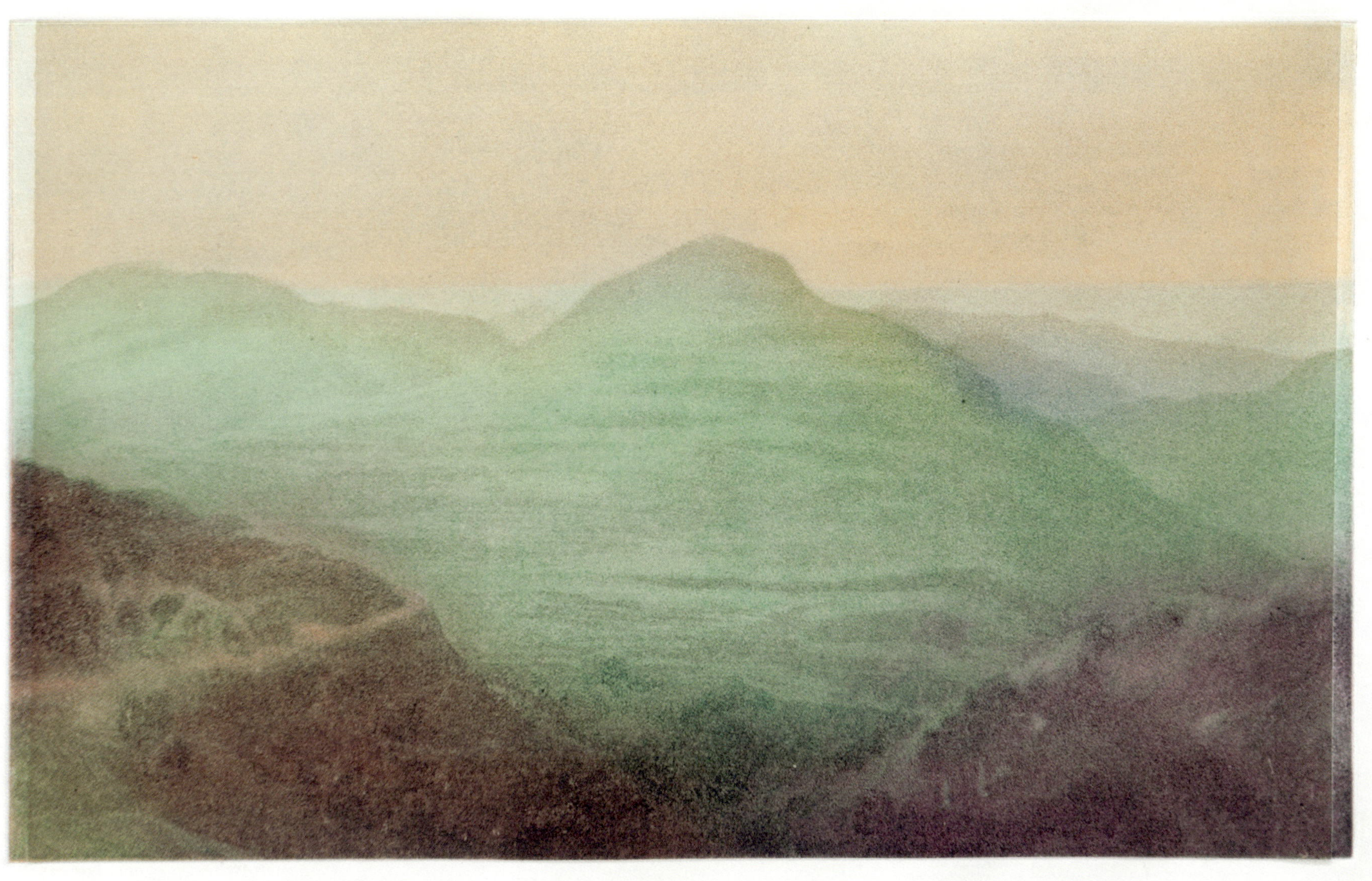

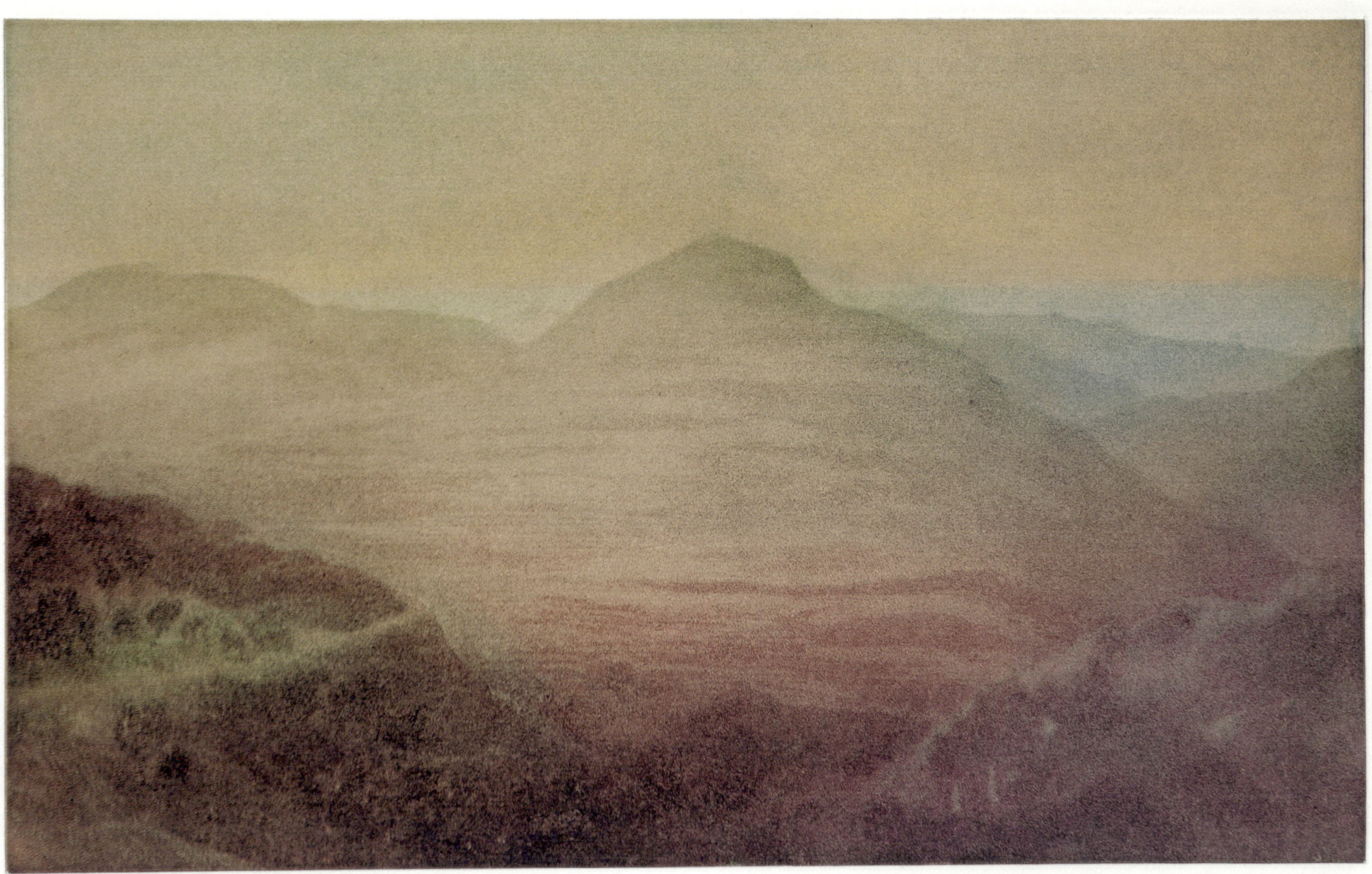

April is the cruellest month, breeding
Lilacs out of the dead land, mixing
Memory and desire, stirring
Dull roots with spring rain.
Winter kept us warm, covering
Earth in forgetful snow, feeding
A little life with dried tubers.[1]

ZW · In TS Eliot's celebrated poem, *The Waste Land* (1922), he describes the burial of the dead, 'breeding', 'mixing', 'stirring' the roots of dormant life. He described April in terms of its brutality, the desolation of the visible winter landscape, yet capable of producing shoots of life from beneath a blanket of snow. I feel that sense of something just below the surface, rousing, in Cathy Wilkes's six-room work.

 A small group of figures surrounds a sepulchral form; small objects are carefully positioned atop and around it. One dear figure perches in proximity. The cloth-covered platform encountered upon first entering Wilkes's 2019 body of work housed in the British Pavilion has a distinctive tiered geometry. This partially references the structure of a tomb.

CW · The work suggests the Assumption, the burial of the body (the subject) when it leaves a state of personal definition and the ascent of the soul into Heaven when it joins the infinite (the object).

What does an artwork such as this mediate? It is a proposal from Wilkes for what purposes art may serve. Its plural functions are not laid bare. It leads us to consider the mysterious place where art moves within us.

1: TS Eliot, *The Waste Land*, in *TS Eliot Selected Poems*, (London: Faber and Faber Limited, 1961), p. 51.

Wilkes's combination of sculptural installation with painting demonstrates a kind of redefinition of genre painting through abstraction; scenes are simultaneously material, with their paint-impregnated surface, and dematerialised, through the inscrutability of subject matter. The sculptures have a painterly quality due to their carefully considered colour and composition, while the paintings possess a physical intensity, built-up during their slow production, through the successive accretion and washing-away of pigment. Her paintings from 2016 show incandescent scenes of fires burning in pale nebulous landscapes (a nuclear winter?), while her recent works are pictures of stillness and dormancy. They seem to show the passage of time in undisturbed natural settings. Their purity and simplicity are presented as if to afford viewers moments of contemplation and reflection.

Through the doctrine of immanence, it is suggested that the spiritual world permeates the mundane. Transcendence, on the other hand, searches through meditation and prayer for a state of divinity elsewhere. The two are bound together in counter-relation.

Returning to Eliot, his later work, *Four Quartets* (1943), interlinks divinity and universality in a series of meditations. *Little Gidding*, the final poem, emphasises salvation and resurrection or rebirth:

> *What we call the beginning is often the end*
> *And to make and end is to make a beginning.*
> *The end is where we start from...*
>
> *We die with the dying:*
> *See, they depart, and we go with them.*

Cathy Wilkes, *Untitled*, 2016
Oil on canvas
76 × 122 × 2.5 cm (30 × 48 × 1 in.)

We are born with the dead:
See, they return, and bring us with them.
The moment of the rose and the moment of the yew-tree
Are of equal duration. A people without history
Is not redeemed from time, for history is a pattern
Of timeless moments.[2]

Eliot uses the paradox of life and death widely in *Little Gidding* to describe the ineffable nature of time, the Universe and the Divine. Biblical allusion also underpins many of Wilkes's works. This is an indelible imprint from her childhood imagination. She references the New Testament, John 1:3, in which all of creation encompassing life and death is a unified whole.

I dignify my creations on the other side of the curtain. On what occasion might I be in such a silence? In the beginning was the Mediation and the Mediation was with God and the Mediation was God. All things were made of it and without it was not anything made that was made. The same was in the beginning with God. All things were made of it and without it was not anything made that was made.[3]

Philosopher and theologian Simone Weil described this kind of communing force between all that is indeterminate and that which we can quantify as the relation between God and 'all that isn't God'. The term 'Word', then, usually designating that which can be defined, takes on an alternate meaning to connote that which is ungraspable. The usual translation 'Word' is replaced by the least inexact translation from the Hebrew; the word 'Mediation'.

Wilkes introduced me to the writings of celebrated Norwegian playwright Jon Fosse. A small package arrived in the mail from her studio manager, Adrien. It contained Fosse's prose

2: TS Eliot, *Little Gidding*, in *Four Quartets*, (London: Faber and Faber Limited, 1959), p. 58.

3: Email correspondence from Cathy Wilkes to Zoé Whitley, received 10 January 2019.

Aliss at the Fire (2003) and Leif Zern's scholarly companion *The Luminous Darkness: The Theatre of Jon Fosse* (2011). Both texts have obliquely brought me a little closer to Wilkes's own oeuvre. Fosse limns coexistence of the living, those yet to be born and those no longer alive. He presents a fragile reconciliation between body and spirit across space and time:

> *that there is a place where children*
> *live together before they are born*
> *where children are in their souls*
> *But they still talk to each other*
> *in their own way*
> *in their own angelic language.*[4]

Wilkes as a visual artist and Fosse as a dramatist both create characterisations that can be fully envisioned at the same time as they evade narrative idiosyncrasy – even down to withholding titles of the work (Wilkes) and the names of the characters (Fosse). Zern offers a guide for what not to expect of Fosse's humans. Audiences expecting characters 'to enter the stage to tell who they are have gone to the wrong play',[5] he affirms. Similarly, Wilkes's modelled or moulded heads hold our attention without giving much away. They are frequently neither male nor female, of indeterminate age (based on height), bearing just enough hallmarks to signify their humanity. Two small indentations for eyes, the vague facial topography of a nose and, sometimes, the curved line of a mouth. Personhood comes into an indistinct soft-focus.

In Fosse's third play, *The Name* (1995), an expectant young father, who remains nameless, envisions an enlarged community populated not only by an unborn choir of angels, but also by the living, the dead, the spectral and those near death. Zern refers to Fosse's personifications

4: Leif Zern, *The Luminous Darkness: The Theatre of Jon Fosse*, (London: Oberon Books, 2011), p. 41.
5: Zern, *The Luminous Darkness*, p. 41.

thus: 'anonymous, interchangeable, impersonal. They all wear a mask that could represent anyone open to an identification different from expected. They often use the pronoun "I" but could just as well say "you".'[6] This kind of evocation of humanity – generalised while encompassing every conceivable stage in the cycle of birth, life and death – is ever-present in Wilkes's work.

If I could disappear, the people I see before me will become perfect in beauty from the very fact that I do not obscure them with my accumulations and my senses.[7] In Omoa I saw a woman in the road, covered in the red and yellow glazes, in the midst of a tempest of wind and water.[8]

[In] this delusion, this dream, visual accuracy and sensitivity became a form of cosmic measuring; divine and aged. But then also [it] obscures everything and is only a form of mediation which has no lasting purpose.[9] I learned from my children; they were mediating with their pictures and their little objects. They relived things and sometimes they rehearsed for the fulfilment of wishes or for loss: they could so easily substitute one thing for another. Sometimes the relation was strong and then sometimes they thought so little of what was left behind.[10]

Wilkes's aesthetic sensitivity and acute visual empathy seem to bestow upon us as viewers an offering. The esoteric notion of 'cosmic measuring', as I understand it, is an awareness of the wondrous unknowability of the observed world. We move through it, armed with empirical data, inured to illusions of clarity and distinctness.

Wilkes applies and searches for language through a system of visual substitutes. Through choice of material and varied techniques, she experiments with a symbolic code of her own making. Within this framework, the symbols stand for more than like-for-like correlations.

6: Zern, *The Luminous Darkness*, p. 41.
7: Email correspondence from Cathy Wilkes to Zoé Whitley, received 10 January 2019.
8: *Cathy Wilkes*, (Liverpool/London: Tate Publishing, 2015), p. 37.
9: Email correspondence from Cathy Wilkes to Zoé Whitley, received 10 January 2019.
10: Email correspondence from Cathy Wilkes to Zoé Whitley, received 30 August 2018.

The nuances of language accommodate few fixed meanings; there are vast chasms between the literal and metaphorical.

The theory of object relations is a name given to ideas about the development of the psyche in relation to experiences in childhood. It proposes that relations both intimate and social become 'objects' in the unconscious mind that are internalised to become part of one's inner world. The first of these is the porous softness and lack of individuation forming the bond of relation between the mother and baby.

A doll is an idea of a being. A sculpture is like a doll – an idea of something in my inner world – a connection with an idea. All sculpture is conceptual, even an imaginary object is like a doll.[11]

In one sense, Wilkes emphasises the fact that a doll isn't a representation of a literal living, breathing, flesh-and-blood child and that any relation to something, physical or non-physical, is connected to our experience of infancy. Yet, while acknowledging this, she can still communicate the metaphorical precariousness of life through an object's physical presence in the work. The artist does not place limitations upon the work. Untethered from the strictures of verbal language, we access it subjectively.

A suggestion of uterine interconnectedness is demonstrated in the swollen tummies borne by the figures in the first room of the exhibition. The circumstances accounting for each distended physique are latent in the work but not belaboured: eagerly anticipated pregnancy; sin and shame of incest; burden of starvation; satiation from gluttonous overindulgence. Or none of these.

A number of Wilkes's earlier works *Non Verbal* (2005) and *Mummy's Here* (2009) seem to show sacred recollections of infancy and early childhood experiences. In these works, even

11: Email correspondence from Cathy Wilkes to Zoé Whitley, received 9 November 2018.

in the absence of a physical body, it is poetically evoked. This conjuring of dematerialised humanity is poignantly expressed by the late Chinese poet and human rights activist Liu Xiaobo. 'Even if I were crushed into powder,' Xiaobo wrote, addressing from prison the love of his life and fellow poet Liu Xia, 'I would still use my ashes to embrace you.'[12] Laureate of the Nobel Peace Prize in 2010, Xiaobo's Nobel lecture was delivered in absentia while serving an 11-year sentence as a political prisoner in China. From his cell, he dedicated the poem *Your Lifelong Prisoner* to his wife, evoking a physical intimacy as intense as the maternal symbiosis of life in the womb.

12: Liu Xiaobo – Nobel Lecture. NobelPrize.org. Nobel Media AB 2019. Fri. 22 March 2019. <https://www.nobelprize.org/prizes/peace/2010/xiaobo/lecture/>

Your Lifelong Prisoner

To Xia

My dear,
I'll never give up the struggle for freedom from the oppressors'
jail, but I'll be your willing prisoner for life.

I'm your lifelong prisoner, my love
I want to live in your dark insides
surviving on the dregs in your blood

inspired by the flow of your estrogen

I hear your constant heartbeat
drop by drop, like melted snow from a mountain stream

if I were a stubborn, million-year rock
you'd bore right through me
drop by drop

day and night

Inside you
I grope in the dark
and use the wine you've drunk
to write poems looking for you
I plead like a deaf man begging for sound
Let the dance of love intoxicate your body

I always feel
your lungs rise and fall when you smoke
in an amazing rhythm
you exhale my toxins
I inhale fresh air to nourish my soul

I'm your lifelong prisoner, my love
like a baby loath to be born
clinging to your warm uterus
you provide all my oxygen
all my serenity

13: Liu Xiaobo, *Your Lifelong Prisoner*,
in Perry Link, Tienchi Martin-Liao and
Liu Xia (eds), *No Enemies, No Hatred:
Selected Essays and Poems*, (Cambridge,
Mass: The Belknap Press of Harvard
University Press, 2012), pp. 174–75.

A baby prisoner
in the depths of your being
unafraid of alcohol and nicotine
the poisons of your loneliness
I need your poisons
need them too much

Maybe as your prisoner
I'll never see the light of day
but I believe
darkness is my destiny
inside you
all is well

The glitter of the outside world
scares me
exhausts me
I focus on
your darkness –
simple and impenetrable[13]

For the past seven years, Wilkes has intentionally left installations, assemblages and exhibitions unnamed. They are deliberately Untitled. She eschews the all-too prescriptive mechanisms by which we often define or seek meanings from cultural engagement. Social activist and feminist writer Selma James offers an expansive, demystifying definition of culture:

The word 'culture' is often used to show that class concepts are narrow, philistine, inhuman. Exactly the opposite is the case... To delimit culture is to reduce it to a decoration of daily life. Culture is plays and poetry about the exploited; ceasing to wear mini-skirts and taking to trousers instead; the clash between the soul of Black Baptism and the guilt and sin of white Protestantism. Culture is also the shrill of the alarm clock that rings at 6 a.m. when a Black woman in London wakes her children to get them ready for the baby-minder. Culture is how cold she feels at the bus stop and then how hot in the crowded bus. Culture is how you feel on Monday morning at eight when you clock in, wishing it was Friday, wishing your life away. Culture is the speed of the line or the weight and smell of dirty hospital sheets, and you meanwhile thinking what to make for tea that night.[14]

Culture is ever bound-up in our lived quotidian realities; it is embodied, everyday life, not a highbrow abstraction removed from human experience. We could each be passengers on that same hot bus, momentarily brought together between our individual destinations. Each trapped in our own subjectivity, we play out our respective lives replete with moments of tedium, of caring for others and requiring care. Wilkes advocates the completely discomfiting position of embracing cultural unknowability. The 2019 exhibition is offered without title and without interpretation. Wilkes appeals for our courage to reject the notion that knowledge is always something we can possess; we are all non-initiates, together we all have equal capacity.

Zoé Whitley
Curator for the British Pavilion 2019 at La Biennale di Venezia

14: Selma James, *Sex, Race and Class – The Perspective of Winning: A Selection of Writings 1952–2011*, (Oakland: PM Press, 2012), p. 95.

Afterword

It is with great pleasure that I introduce the exhibition and accompanying catalogue by
Cathy Wilkes for the 58th International Art Exhibition – La Biennale di Venezia. The British
Council has been commissioning exhibitions for the British Pavilion ever since 1937, when it
took responsibility for the historic, neo-classical former tea house, presenting its first exhibition
there a year later.

We are delighted that our selection committee chose for the Biennale Arte 2019 the Belfast-
born, Glasgow-based Cathy Wilkes, to represent the UK with an exhibition of entirely new works,
created especially for the British Pavilion. Her exhibition is a unique and powerful contribution
to the Biennale Arte 2019 and to the British Pavilion's long and illustrious history.

Since the late 1990s, Wilkes has built a considerable reputation for her sculptural installations of profound and mysterious intensity, which often evoke interiors and places of loss.
Her work is tender, intimate and autobiographical, yet universal. The selection committee chose
her for the fierce integrity of her work, as well as for her growing international following.
Her distinctive and highly personal sculptural installations evoke everyday rituals, while alluding
to existential questions at the core of human existence, triggering complex new meanings and
atmospherics within the grand domestic architecture of the British Pavilion.

Participation in major cultural events such as La Biennale di Venezia is essential for
continuing international dialogue and exchange, ensuring that cultural relations are at the
heart of the UK's cultural, educational and people-to-people connections with the other
countries of Europe and, just as importantly, with the rest of the world. Artists, curators and
organisations join a global community when they exhibit at the Biennale, fostering new
international relationships and collaborations in a spirit of shared enterprise and endeavour.

From 2019 onwards, it is vital that Europe's creative sectors continue to strengthen collaborative working in order to respond to their shared future challenges.

For the Biennale Arte 2019, the British Council created, for the first time, an opportunity for a UK-based, mid-career curator, selected via an open call process, to curate the British Pavilion, thereby widening access to international working for UK visual arts professionals. The successful candidate, Dr Zoé Whitley, has worked tirelessly alongside the artist and project team to realise the exhibition and we are grateful for her dedication and attention to detail throughout the collaborative process, which has been both productive and enjoyable, and for her insightful text in this publication.

We are deeply grateful to Cathy Wilkes for her meticulously crafted and visionary concept and her team for their commitment and hard work in realising this memorable and moving exhibition. We would also like to thank everyone at The Modern Institute for their invaluable support and collaboration in delivering the project and our Venice Fellows for invigilating.

The exhibition and its related activities would not have been possible without the support and involvement of numerous collaborators and partners. We are particularly indebted to our individual donors and sponsors who have shown such passion in their support; most notably Therme Group, Art Fund, Donald Porteous and Outset x Mazzoleni.

Finally, this exhibition represents a huge amount of teamwork across numerous parts of the British Council. I wish to thank my colleagues for their passion, professionalism and hard work in bringing the exhibition, catalogue and supporting elements into being.

Emma Dexter
Commissioner for the British Pavilion at La Biennale di Venezia

All colour plates:

Cathy Wilkes
Polymer gravure / polymer gravure
with chine-collé
Photo: Patrick Jameson
Courtesy of the artist and The Modern
Institute/Toby Webster Ltd, Glasgow

Cathy Wilkes
Born 1966, Dundonald, Belfast,
Northern Ireland; lives and works in
Glasgow, Scotland.

Dr Zoé Whitley
Senior Curator at the Hayward Gallery,
London.

Cathy Wilkes
British Council commission for the
58th International Art Exhibition –
La Biennale di Venezia,
from 11 May to 24 November 2019

https://venicebiennale.britishcouncil.org/

Commissioner for the British Pavilion
Emma Dexter
Deputy Commissioner
Gemma Hollington
Curator
Dr. Zoé Whitley
Visual Arts Workshop and Technical Manager
Marcus Alexander
Visual Arts Workshop Deputy Manager
David Garnett
Touring Exhibitions Manager
Rohan Stephens
Touring Exhibitions Assistant
Rebekka Deighton
Director of Development
Deborah Myers
Development Officer
Amy Jakar
Marketing Manager Visual Arts
Cherelle Cunningham
Fellowships Manager
Genevieve Marciniak
Lead Content and Digital Marketing Manager
Jane Fletcher
Senior Press Officer
Hayley Willis
Events Officer
Laura McDonald
Venice Team Assistants
Emily Medd, Jacob De Munnik
Director, British Council Italy
Paul Sellers

Relationships and Projects Manager,
British Council Italy
Alison Driver

British Pavilion Maintenance Supervisor
Piero Morello
British Pavilion Electrical Consultant
Cesare de Rossi

Pr Consultant
Scott & Co.

Film Production
Cultureshock Media

Venice Biennale 2019 Selection Committee
David A. Bailey, Director, International
Curators Forum
Fiona Bradley, Director, The Fruitmarket
Gallery, Edinburgh
Anne Barlow, Director, Tate St Ives
Katy Freer, Exhibitions Officer, Glynn
Vivian Art Gallery, Swansea
Martin Herbert, Writer and Critic
Melanie Keen, Director, Iniva, London
Hugh Mulholland, Senior Curator,
The Mac, Belfast
Sarah Munro, Director, BALTIC Centre
for Contemporary Art, Gateshead
Joe Scotland, Director, Studio Voltaire,
London

Acknowledgements
Eva Abercromby
David Frazier
Dan Griffiths
Andrew Hamilton
Steve Higgins
Adrien Howard
Xavier Hufkens
Patrick Jameson
Torsten Lauschmann
Dave MacAllister
Darren Rhymes
Alicia Riccio
Ellie Royle
Jonathan Snee
Billy Teasdale
Hester Van Royen
Thom Wall
Toby Webster
Arne Wern

Special thanks to
Thumbprint Editions, London
Peter Kosowicz
Raquel Martinez

Everyone at The Modern Institute/
Toby Webster Ltd, Glasgow and
Xavier Hufkens, Brussels.

Sponsored by

THERME
GROUP™

Supported by

Art Fund_

With thanks to the Exhibition Supporters' Circle
Donald Porteous

Emma and Fred Goltz
Rennie Collection
Susan and Larry Marx
Xavier Hufkens
Jill and Peter Kraus

Pamela J. Joyner and Alfred J. Giuffrida

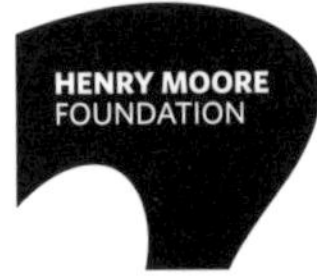

Pavilion Patrons
OUtSet. x MAZZOLENI

The Lord Browne of Madingley

Zabludowicz Collection
Belinda de Gaudemar
Midge and Simon Palley

British Pavilion Fellowship Supporters
David Roberts Art Foundation
Sarah L. Elson

Hospitality Sponsor

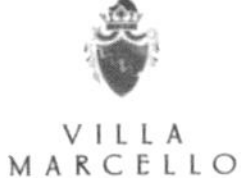

VILLA
MARCELLO

The British Council would like to thank our
British Pavilion Fellowship partners
Arts University Bournemouth
a space arts
Birkbeck, University of London
University of Bolton
Bristol Museum & Art Gallery
University of Cambridge
London Metropolitan University (Cass)
Central Saint Martins, UAL
Canterbury Christ Church University
Coventry University
University of Cumbria
University of Derby
Falmouth University
Firstsite Colchester
Golden Thread Gallery
Kettle's Yard
Kingston University, University of London
Lancaster University
London College of Communication, UAL
University of Leicester
University of Liverpool
Loughborough University
Manchester School of Art
New Contemporaries
Nottingham Contemporary
Nottingham Trent University
Queen Margaret University
University of Portsmouth
Plymouth College of Art
Royal College of Art
The Ruskin School of Art
University of Salford
South London Gallery
University of the West of England
Wysing Arts Centre

Designed by Yvonne Quirmbach
Edited by Phoebe Adler
Production Manager Sarah McLaughlin

Printed in Italy by Verona Libri